TornabuoniArt

ITALIA MINIMAL

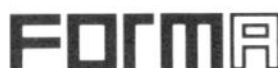

Editorial project
Forma Edizioni srl
Florence, Italy
redazione@formaedizioni.it
www.formaedizioni.it

Editorial director
Laura Andreini

Editorial coordination
Quentin Laurent

Editorial staff
Maria Giulia Caliri
Livia D'Aliasi

Graphic design
Laura Maltinti
Isabella Peruzzi

Translations
Quentin Laurent
Jenna Romagnolo
Alice de Sanctis

Photolithography
LAB di Gallotti
Giuseppe Fulvio
Firenze, Italia

Photo Credits
© Fondazione Burri p. 11
© Fondazione Piero Manzoni pp. 24, 25
© Nataly Maier p. 10
© Ugo Mulas pp. 8, 13
© Pinacoteca di Brera, Milan p. 10
© Tornabuoni Art pp. 17-23, 27-55, 62-63

First edition: October 2020

This catalogue is published on the occasion of the exhibition

ITALIA Minimal
Tornabuoni Art Paris
16 avenue Matignon 75008 Paris
22 October - 22 December 2020

Project by
Tornabuoni Art Paris

Organisation
Tornabuoni Art Paris and Florence

Text
Ilaria Bignotti

Special thanks to all the lenders, especially Alighiero Boetti heirs, Fondazione Piero Manzoni and Roberto Casamonti.

We would like to thank all of those who contributed to the realization of this catalogue: Germana Agnetti, Ilaria Bignotti, Agata Boetti, Rosalia Pasqualino di Marineo, Federico Sardella and the staff of Tornabuoni Art Paris and Florence, in particular Isabella Capolei, Isabella Lastrucci, Quentin Laurent and Alice de Sanctis.

pp. 62-63
Alighiero Boetti
Catasta, 1967-92
12 elements in Eternit
187 × 150 × 150 cm /
73 ⅝ × 59 × 59 in
(detail)

ITALIA MINIMAL

Tornabuoni Art launches its new Paris gallery on 22 October 2020 with the *ITALIA Minimal* exhibition: carefully selected masterpieces created by the undisputed leaders of visual experimentation between the late 1950s and '70s: Vincenzo Agnetti, Alighiero Boetti, Agostino Bonalumi, Alberto Burri, Enrico Castellani, Mario Ceroli, Gianni Colombo, Dadamaino, Lucio Fontana, Emilio Isgrò, Jannis Kounellis, Sergio Lombardo, Piero Manzoni, Paolo Scheggi and Giuseppe Uncini.

As the title of the exhibition suggests, the post-war work by these Italian masters – the show includes non-Italians who worked in Italy, such as Jannis Kounellis, as well as hybrid artist Lucio Fontana who was Argentinian and Italian but worked in Milan – is interpreted through the lens of Minimalism: a definition which, although traditionally linked to art from overseas, can offer an interesting insight into Italian culture between the 1960s and '70s, highlighting affinities, points of contact and diversion between these figures and American experiences.

Suffice it to say that Donald Judd described Enrico Castellani as a precursor to "his" Minimalism, and the founder of Azimuth himself – although he expressed his distaste for any "ism", or defined artistic movement – brought attention to the shared efforts of Italian and American artists to abandon everything spurious, decorative, narrative, and ideological, in the name of a tension towards the essential and absolute. This tension was resolved in the precise choice of the artistic object's elements and constitutive parts, such as colour, space, material and the gesture that shapes the definition of form, in full contact, guarded and tense with the creation of the work, in the aspiration towards that essential which necessarily passes through the sublimation of the accidental and the fleeting.[1]

Being an artist means working without any *pathos* or yielding, but with that "rigour", as Agostino Bonalumi pointed out back in 1975, "which means a push

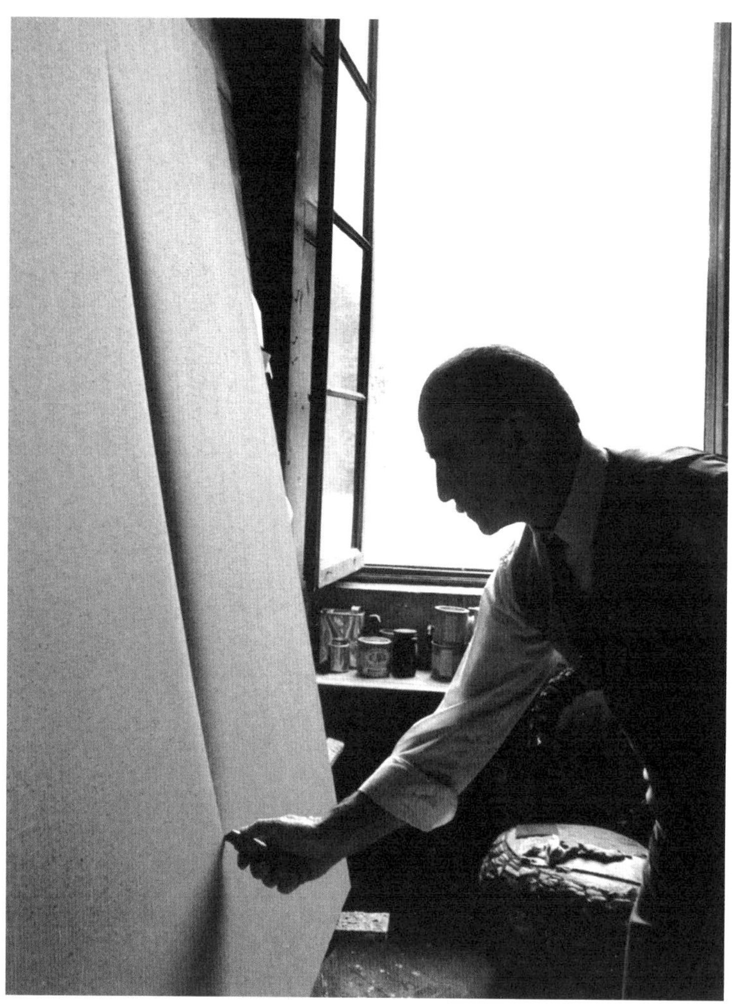

Lucio Fontana,
L'attesa, Milan, 1964

1. S. Indrisek, "Enrico Castellani. One of Minimalism's Fathers", in *Blouin Artinfo*, 7 October 2014, no page. A version of this article was also published in the October issue of *Modern Painters* magazine.

2. A. Bonalumi, "Rigore e ricerca", in *Opera grafica e osservazioni di Agostino Bonalumi*, exh. cat. (Milan, Galleria Bon à tirer / grafica, 5 June 1975), no page; subsequently in *Bonalumi*, (Florence, Galleria d'Arte La Piramide, 14 October - 6 November 1975), no page.

3. A. Bonito Oliva, "Minimalia. Una linea italiana del XX secolo", in *Minimalia. Da Giacomo Balla a...*, ed. by A. Bonito Oliva, exh. cat., (Venice, Palazzo Querini Dubois, June - September 1997), Bocca Edizioni, Vicenza, 1997, p. XIII.

towards deeper study, giving the research the sense of a vertical development that in turn signifies the growth of the research on oneself (internal attention exercise)."[2]

Italian artists interpreted the ideas of Minimalism in protean and playful ways which Tornabuoni Art is now presenting to the public: these works combine a spirit of experimentation and formality, a tension between analysis and improvisation, characterized by radical innovation and harmonious freshness.

This was also emphasized, twenty-one years ago, by Achille Bonito Oliva in the great *Minimalia* exhibition, first held in Venice in 1997 and then in Rome in 1998 with the title *Minimalia. Da Giacomo Balla a...*, and from October 1999 to January 2000 at the Museum of Modern Art PS1 in New York, with the title *Minimalia. An Italian 20th Century Vision*: many of the artists who were included at the time now have works on show at Tornabuoni Art: Agnetti, Burri, Castellani, Ceroli, Colombo, Dadamaino, Fontana, Kounellis, Lombardo, Manzoni and Uncini.

"While North American Minimalism always borders on pure geometrical reduction, the standard of the skyscraper and simple form, it is possible to trace an Italian 'Minimalia', capable of retaining complex features in the rigour of its forms that cannot be reduced to pure geometry," Achille Bonito Oliva wrote in the catalogue, stressing that for an Italian artist geometry is not dogma, but the "prolific field of irregular reasoning that likes to asymmetrically develop its own principles, adopting the surprise, the emotion."[3]

In 1964, Paolo Scheggi, one of the artists on show at Tornabuoni Art, describing the construction method based on the circle and square of his *Intersuperfici*, explains: "The instability of the perception of objects and the development of research constitute the operative method which, rejecting every intention and attribute of art, tends towards a greater cognitive dialectic without naturalistic extractions."[4]

Italian art, compared to American Minimalism, is intended as an "open examination", a "glaring and progressive reflection [...] of a different visibility that is produced from the work's 'cosa mentale' (mental thing)."[5] Leonardo Da Vinci had written about it five centuries earlier, with regard to painting, initiating a very long history of art that extends from Renaissance Humanism to Italian 20th-century research. This is a history that arose in the context of 15th-century art, the bearer of an "initial form that progressively develops through modular moments that multiply, without repetition, the initial moment [...]"[6]: Italian art also developed thanks to the Renaissance invention of perspective, which established a new way of portraying and of experiencing objects in space.

Bonito Oliva referred to Paolo Uccello's painting *The Battle of San Romano* as an iconic example of Renaissance perspective in art. I would like to point to a modern example: a crucial exhibition of Italian art in the 1960s, *Lo spazio dell'immagine*, (The Space of the Image) – an homage to Lucio Fontana – held

4. P. Scheggi, "Proposte sul cerchio. Dieci Intersuperfici curve bianche", June 1964, in *Paolo Scheggi. Catalogue Raisonné*, ed. by L. M. Barbero, scientific coordination by I. Bignotti, Skira, Milan, 2016, p. 154.

5. A. Bonito Oliva, "Minimalia. Una linea italiana del XX secolo", *op. cit.*, pp. XIII, XIV, XXVI.

6. Ivi, p. XIII.

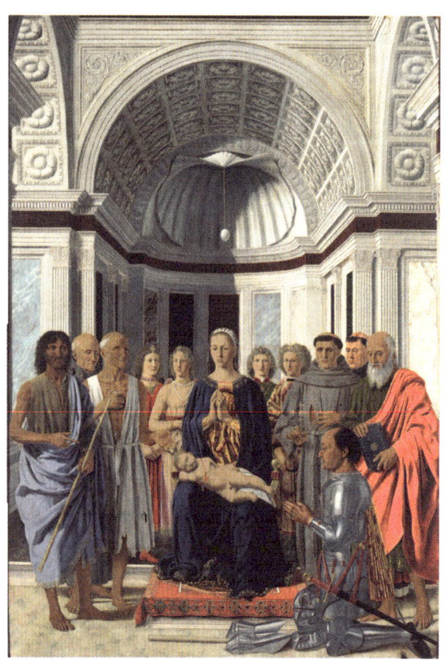

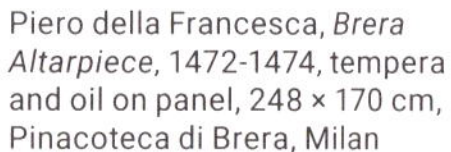

Piero della Francesca, *Brera Altarpiece*, 1472-1474, tempera and oil on panel, 248 × 170 cm, Pinacoteca di Brera, Milan

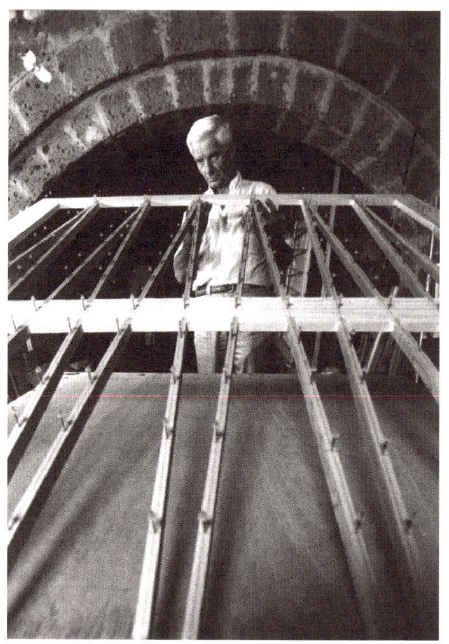

Enrico Castellani in his studio, Cellano, Italy, 1987

at Palazzo Trinci in Foligno in 1967, which displayed a reproduction of the egg from Piero della Francesca's *Brera Altarpiece*[7] alongside *Environments* by Agostino Bonalumi, Enrico Castellani, Mario Ceroli, Gianni Colombo and Paolo Scheggi,[8] artists currently on display at Tornabuoni Art.

Placed behind the Virgin, Piero's egg descends from a taut thread in the centre of an inverted shell, which is also the apse of the entire composition of architecture and sacred figures. At the back of a windowless room, it is lit like Mary's head and seems to hang perpendicularly above her. Light is used in an intellectual, non-naturalistic way, blending the shapes of objects with those of the characters represented.
Piero's egg: a perfect and closed, absolute and metaphysical form, the measure and reason of the entire pictorial structure that supports and "makes" the *Brera Altarpiece*; but also an icon of life that is fertile, germinating, unexpected. An image of great Italian design that was chosen at the height of the 1960s as the

7. The Altarpiece with the *Sacra Conversazione*, commissioned to Piero della Francesca by Federico da Montefeltro, the lord of Urbino, to celebrate the birth of his male heir Guidubaldo in 1472 and to commemorate the death of his wife Battista Sforza, who died in childbirth

8. *Lo spazio dell'immagine*, texts by U. Apollonio, G. C. Argan, P. Bucarelli, M. Calvesi, G. Celant, G. De Marchis, G. Dorfles, C. Finch, U. Kultermann, G. Marchiori, L. V. Masini, exh. cat., (Foligno, Palazzo Trinci, 2 July - 1 October 1967), Artegrafica, Venice, 1967. The invited artists were: Getulio Alviani, Alberto Biasi, Agostino Bonalumi, Davide Boriani (Gruppo T), Enrico Castellani, Mario Ceroli, Gianni Colombo (Gruppo T), Gabriele de Vecchi (Gruppo T), Luciano Fabro, Tano Festa, Piero Gilardi, Gino Marotta, Eliseo Mattiacci, Romano Notari, Pino Pascali, Michelangelo Pistoletto, Gruppo MID, Gruppo ENNE and

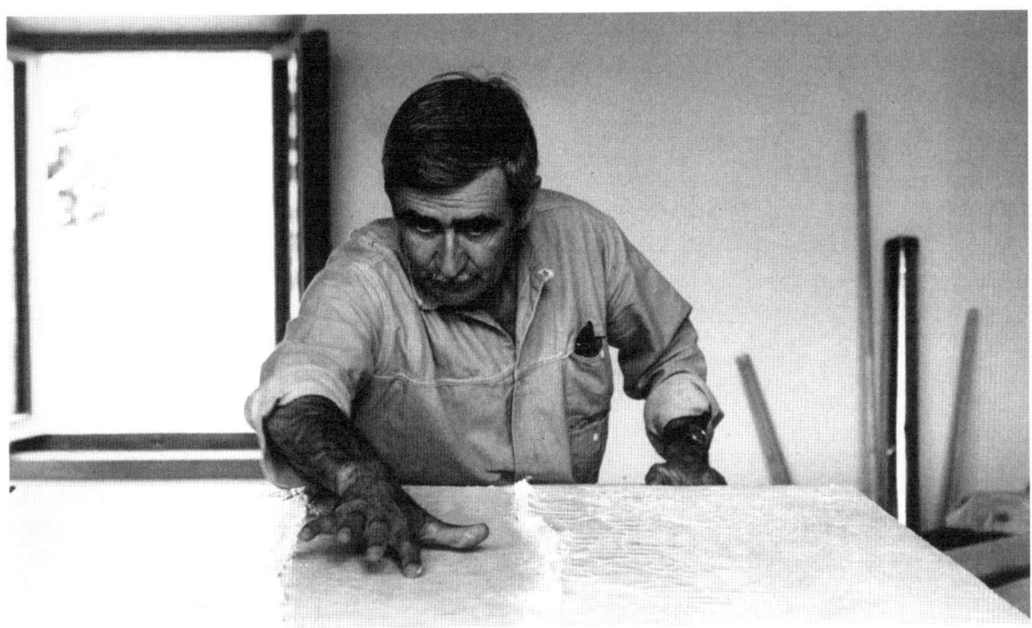

Alberto Burri at work, 1973 ca.

ideal symbol to narrate the most important visual investigations as they extended their work into the environment to create a more interactive relationship with the spectator.

Again in 1967, at the San Marino Biennale devoted to the *Nuove tecniche di immagine* (New Image Techniques) theme in the *Astrazione oggettuale e costruzione dell'oggetto* (Object Abstraction and Construction) section, the works of Italian artists Castellani and Scheggi and the American artists Robert Indiana and Frank Stella were exhibited together, forming a dialogue: united by the common investigation into a "geometry aligned with the notion of Object [...] a pure idea reconstructed by hand. Spatial encumbrance is a symptom of a vision of the world that enters triumphantly into the world. And abstractionism is no longer understood in the historical sense (intuition, expression, didactics and imagination), but as visual research, as optical persuasion,"[9] Maurizio Fagiolo stressed in the catalogue.

Paolo Scheggi. There were two special invitations: Ettore Colla with an exhibition of outdoor sculptures, accompanied in the catalogue by a critical text by Palma Bucarelli (pp. 42-49), and Lucio Fontana with *Ambiente spaziale a luce nera*, in the catalogue with a critical text by Giulio Carlo Argan (pp. 51-60).

9. M. Fagiolo Dell'Arco, "Nuove frontiere dell'immagine" in *VI Biennale Internazionale di San Marino. Nuove Tecniche d'Immagine*, ed. by S. Pinto and P. Manzù, texts by G. C. Argan, P. Bucarelli, M. Calvesi, M. Fagiolo Dall'Arco, C. Jürgen, O. Hahn, San Marino, (Palazzo dei Congressi, 15 July - 30 September 1967), Alfieri Edizioni d'Arte, Venice, 1967, p. 22. The participants in the *Astrazione oggettuale e costruzione dell'oggetto* section were as follows: Adzak, Aricò, Barker, Bauermeister, Brunelle, Castellani, Gandini, Grosse, Hinman, Indiana, Insley, Kiender, Micus, Oldenburg, Sanejouand, Scheggi, Schreib and Stella.

Let's look at these works today: they are messages of a form of minimalism that is not a pure arithmetic procedure, but a constant examination of the relationships between surface, size, material, space and colour: a form of minimalism that is open to life and warmed by a Mediterranean sense of inventiveness and spontaneity, the fruit of Italian intuition.

It was suggested twenty-one years ago in the exhibition *Minimalia*, it is today pursued by Tornabuoni Art in *ITALIA Minimal*: in the past two decades, marked by momentous traumas that are radically transforming relationships, contexts and balances between man, space and time, we ask art to help us understand our dimension in the world, amidst virtual situations, disrupted relationships, economic crises and political upheavals. We also do this by interpreting and reinterpreting the 1960s and '70s as paradigmatic periods in which Italian artists fused objectification with experience, exploration of form with the potential of space, light and air, looking through an imaginary telescope that could unite the Renaissance and the moon, the absolute metaphysical and the iridescent accident, within a movement towards a new, pure sensibility, mindful, also, of formal asceticism from Malevič to Brancusi to Arp, of manifesto constructions from Mondrian to Bauhaus to Constructivism.

The pursuit of the absolute is translated into an attempt to condense the lowest common denominator of the world's things in the work, that is, to find the pure form, beyond any possible condition and contamination: sublime perfection, so exact and absolute that it is truly dizzying.
This is why, today, we have an increasing need of it and we return to looking at the works of these pioneers of visual language: they give us new eyes to do so.

ITALIA Minimal presents this compelling and passionate research: cherished and offered to the eye in Piero Manzoni's unstable and lively *Achrome*, in Lucio Fontana's open wounds on the new; in Castellani's restless textures and in Bonalumi's inside-out tensions; coveted and chased on the edges of the openings that penetrate and overlook Scheggi's *Intersuperfici* and in the cracks in Burri's coruscating and recomposed material; declared by Agnetti's unattainable illusions and in Boetti's secret measurements. Research that is repeated again in Boetti, unfolds in Colombo, is articulated in Dadamaino and honed in Lombardo; it hits us in Kounellis, cages us in Uncini and warms us in Ceroli.

Simplifying is complex: a total choice. Italian minimalist artists stand in the ring of art – and life – as heavyweights.

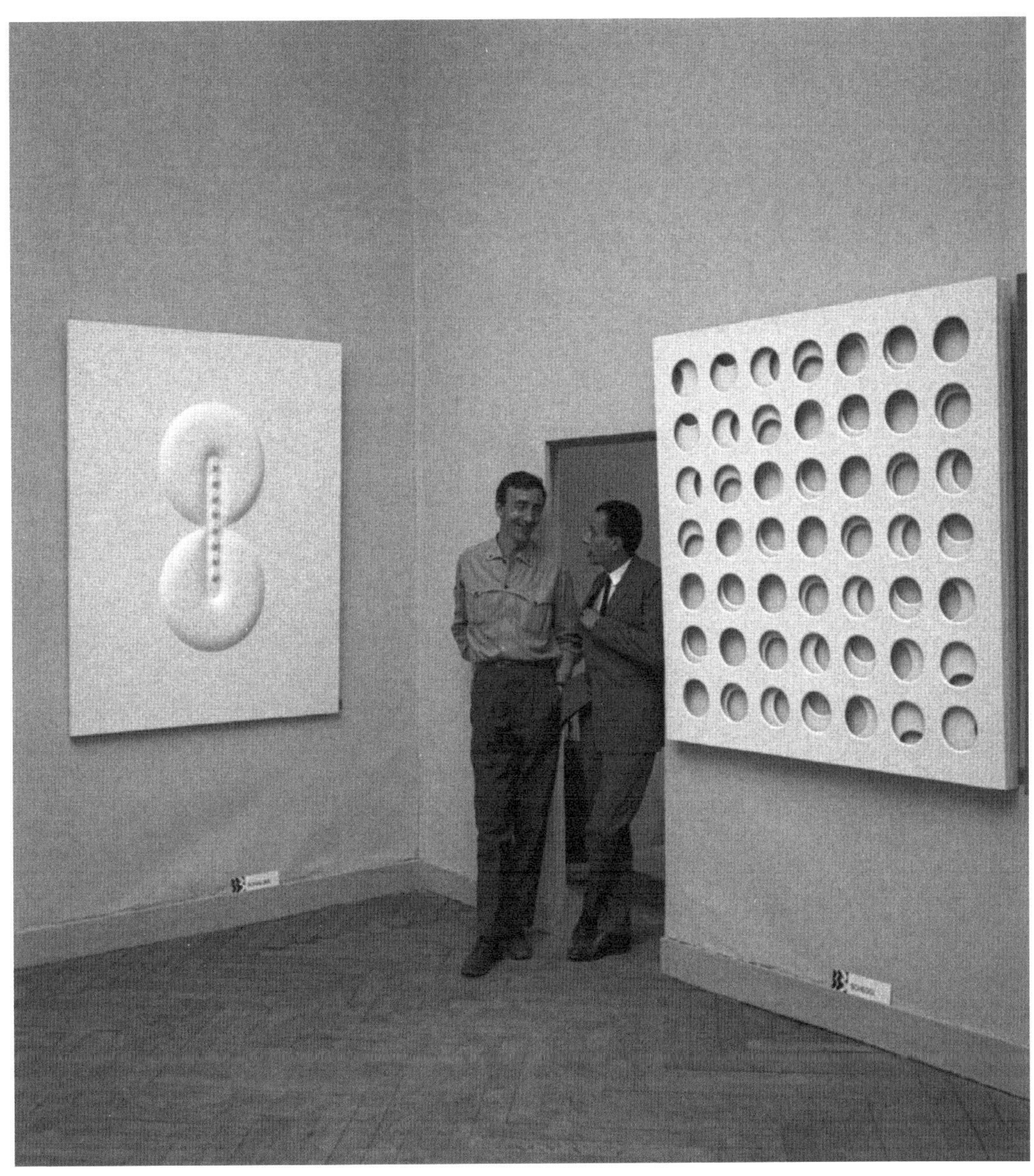

Agostino Bonalumi and
Paolo Scheggi in their exhibition
room at the Venice Biennale, 1966

ARTWORKS

Lucio Fontana
Concetto spaziale, attese, 1965
water-based paint on canvas
100 × 81 cm / 39 ⅜ × 31 ⅞ in

"I do not want to make a painting. I want to open space, to create a new dimension for art, to connect it to the cosmos, as it stretches, in its infinity, beyond the flat surface of the image."

– **LUCIO FONTANA**

– "Manifest of spatial art" 1965, in Enrico Crispolti, *Lucio Fontana. Catalogue Raisonné*, Vol. I, La Connaissance, Brussels, 1974, p. 7.

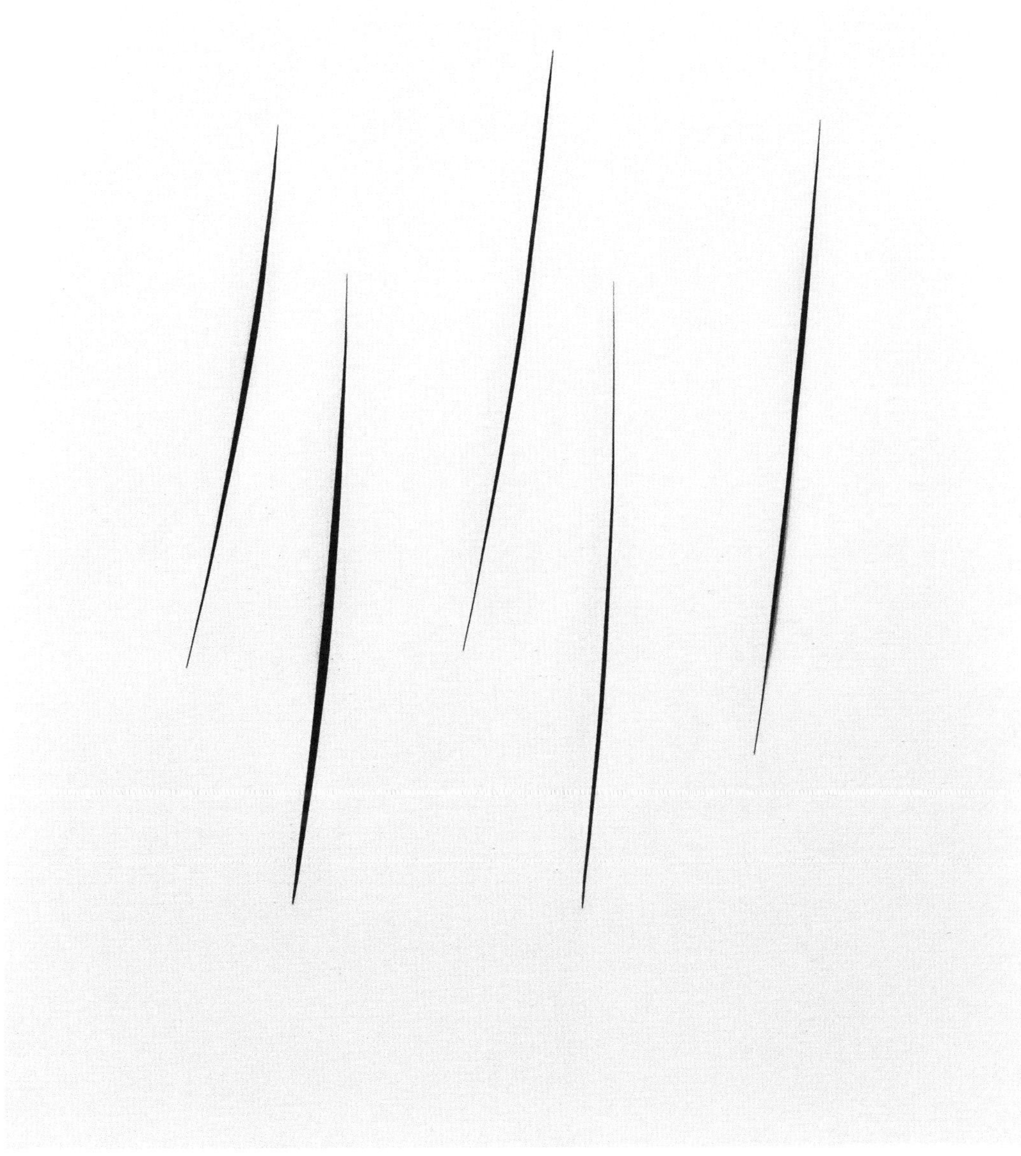

Lucio Fontana
Concetto spaziale, attese, 1967
water-based paint on canvas
61 × 50 cm / 24 × 19 ¾ in

"The choice of purification and the ideal moment in the existence of the *Tagli* (Slashes) appears to come with the advance of monochromy on the canvas. The monochrome background takes them to a new dimension, with a new role. From the objectifying concept of the monochrome surface and thus from the 'body' adopted by the canvas, the *Tagli* increasingly appear as a carefully thought-out and ordered structure, to the point that they can even cut through the surface a number of times, along diagonal or tilted lines, or even slightly arched. As Crispolti writes: 'we begin to see a decisive, characteristic use of monochrome in the new cycle of works, together with a desire to give order to the slashes as primary, elementary structures that are exquisitely calibrated'."

– LUCA MASSIMO BARBERO

– "L'invenzione del segno : Lucio Fontana", in *Lucio Fontana*, exhibition catalogue (London, Tornabuoni Art, 8 October - 5 December 2015), Forma Edizioni, Florence, 2015, p. 66.

Alberto Burri
Plastica, 1963
plastic and combustion
on aluminium frame
98 × 74 cm / 38 5/8 × 29 1/8 in

"... The *Plastiche* [...] represent a fresh and dazzling departure. They were carried out between 1961 and the early months of 1962, and in a way they represent the culmination of all Burri's previous experiments. But in the direct line which leads from the *Gobbi* through the *Combustione* and the *Ferri* to the *Plastiche*, they constitute an astonishing novelty."

– CESARE BRANDI

– *Burri*, exhibition catalogue, ed. by Cesare Brandi, (Rome, Marlborough Galleria d'Arte, December 1962 - January 1963), Editalia, Rome, 1962.

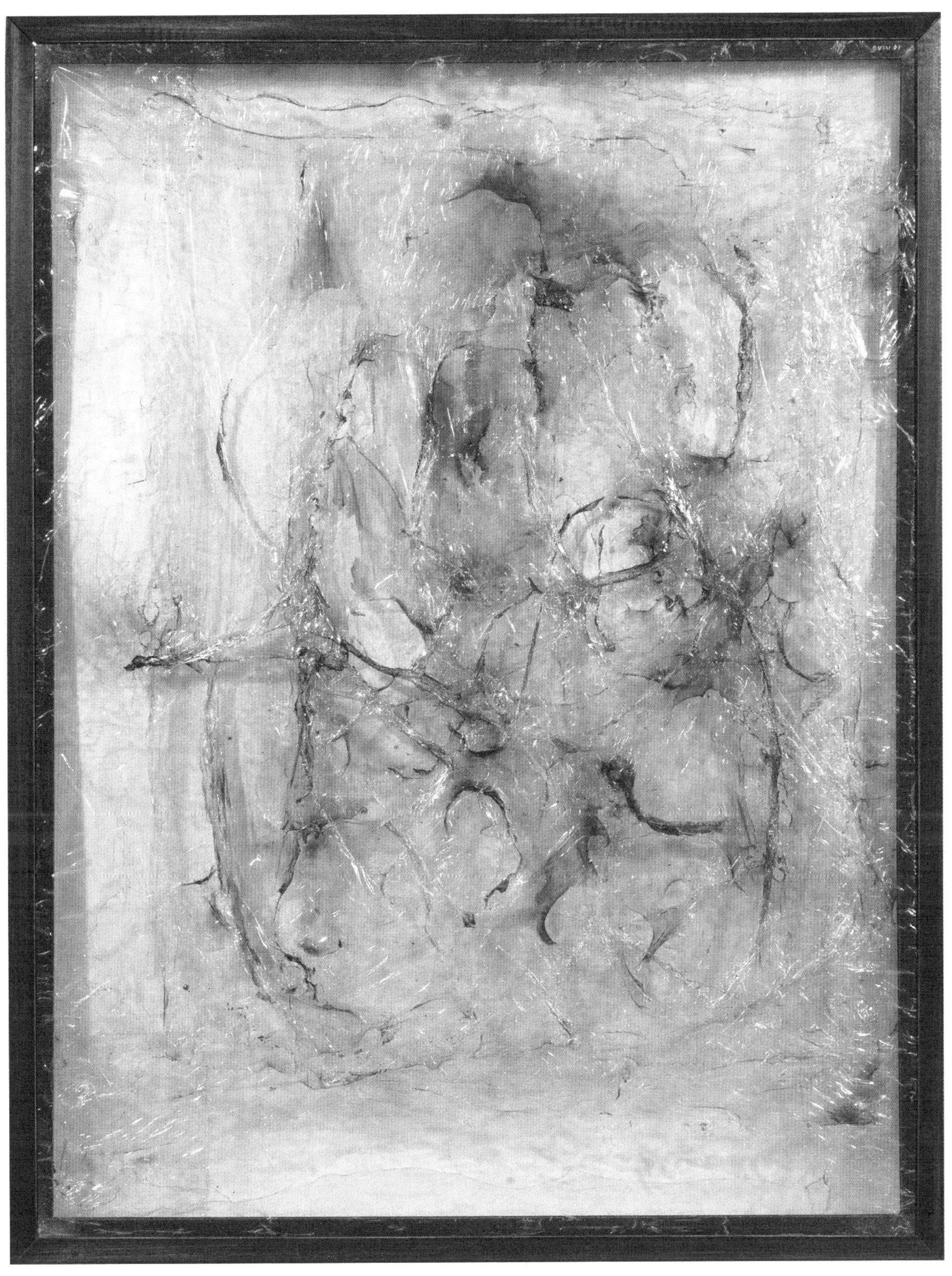

Piero Manzoni
Achrome, 1958-59
China-clay on canvas
70 × 91 cm / 27 ½ × 35 ⅞ in

Piero Manzoni
Linea m 15,81, September 1959
ink on paper and cardboard tube
31 × ø 5,5 cm / 12 ¼ × ø 2 ⅛ in
Fondazione Piero Manzoni, Milan

Piero Manzoni
Achrome, 1960 c.
cotton wool in squares
40 × 30 cm / 15 ¾ × 11 ¾ in
Fondazione Piero Manzoni, Milan

"Piero Manzoni did the first *Achromes* in 1956. In them, the artist made a blank slate of all existential questions and interests, and began to consider the painting as an 'area of liberty', which initially freed itself from all chromatic or figurative implications, becoming *Achrome*, without colour, a mute surface and canvas, freed of all allusive and descriptive, allegorical and symbolic input. The *Achrome* establishes itself as a self-signifying sign, it eliminates all autobiography and does away with the personal mystique of the artist. It recognises, in its act of being there, the individuality of the canvas and the material that covers it, endowing their 'birth' with a fundamental value. The *Achrome* 'colourless', is an entity in its elementary state, it neither speaks nor explains, it is not a tool, but a field of limitless possibilities of life. The *Achrome* is the objective life, it cannot be considered as an unit and moment; and as the homogeneous succession of a single being that develops in time and space."

– **GERMANO CELANT**

– *Piero Manzoni*, catalogue raisonné, ed. by Germano Celant, vol. 1, Prearo Editore, Milan, 1975.

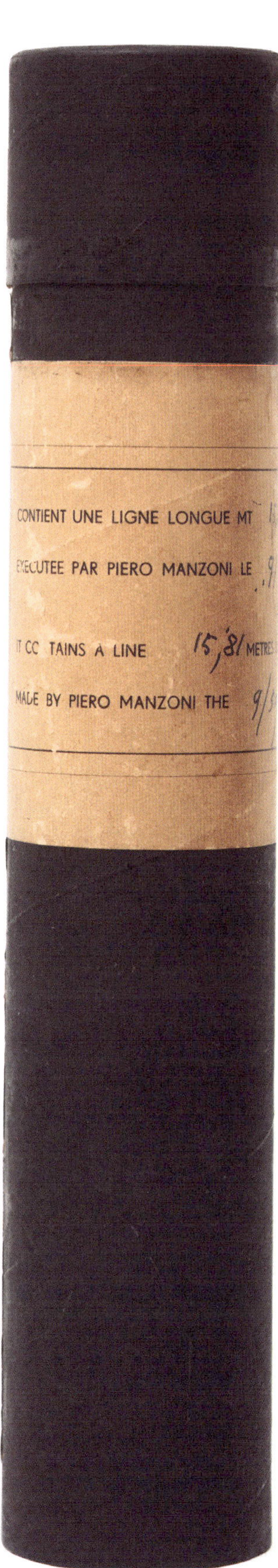
CONTIENT UNE LIGNE LONGUE MT
EXECUTEE PAR PIERO MANZONI LE
IT CC TAINS A LINE 15,81 METRES
MADE BY PIERO MANZONI THE

Enrico Castellani
Superficie bianca n°5, 1964
tempera on shaped canvas
146 × 114 × 30 cm / 57 ½ × 44 ⅞ × 11 ¾ in

"Castellani's œuvre redefines its purpose in a quest that transcends the finality of each of its models. It inaugurates a new destiny for painting, as Donald Judd didn't fail to notice. In the famous text he published in 1965 and entitled *Specific Objects*, he acknowledges an art that would be 'neither painting nor sculpture' and therefore, a redefinition of the perceptive and conceptual schemes that had been, until him, the foundation of aesthetic ambition. By rejecting the dominant principles of the art of the 1950's, Castellani participated in this desire to refute the idea that painting has to do with gesture and action, and established the foundations of an objectivist art. I will add that Castellani redefines the relationships between *ars* and *technè* by the mastery – in the companion sense of the word – with which he builds, constructs, and assembles his object."

– **BERNARD BLISTÈNE**

– *Enrico Castellani*, exhibition catalogue, ed. by Bernard Blistène, (Paris, Tornabuoni Art, 14 October - 15 December 2011), Forma Edizioni, Florence, 2011, p. 44.

Enrico Castellani
Superficie bianca, 1999
acrylic on shaped canvas
150 × 200 cm / 59 × 78 ¾ in

"The expression 'Minimalism' is like all the other 'isms' a mediatic invention to simplify the analysis of cultural events, which came to my knowledge when its meaning was already widely spread and applied to all human activities.
The simplistic definition never interested me.
I have been acquainted with Donald Judd's work independently from the label that defined him and I have appreciated him because I recognized in his method the same radicality that conducted my research, which comes from the necessity to relieve painting from an overload of fallacious elements (literary, descriptive, ideological etc.) to restore its essentiality."

– ENRICO CASTELLANI

– S. Indrisek, "Enrico Castellani. One of Minimalism's Fathers", in *Blouin Artinfo*, 7 October 2014, no page. A version of this article was also published in the October issue of *Modern Painters* magazine.

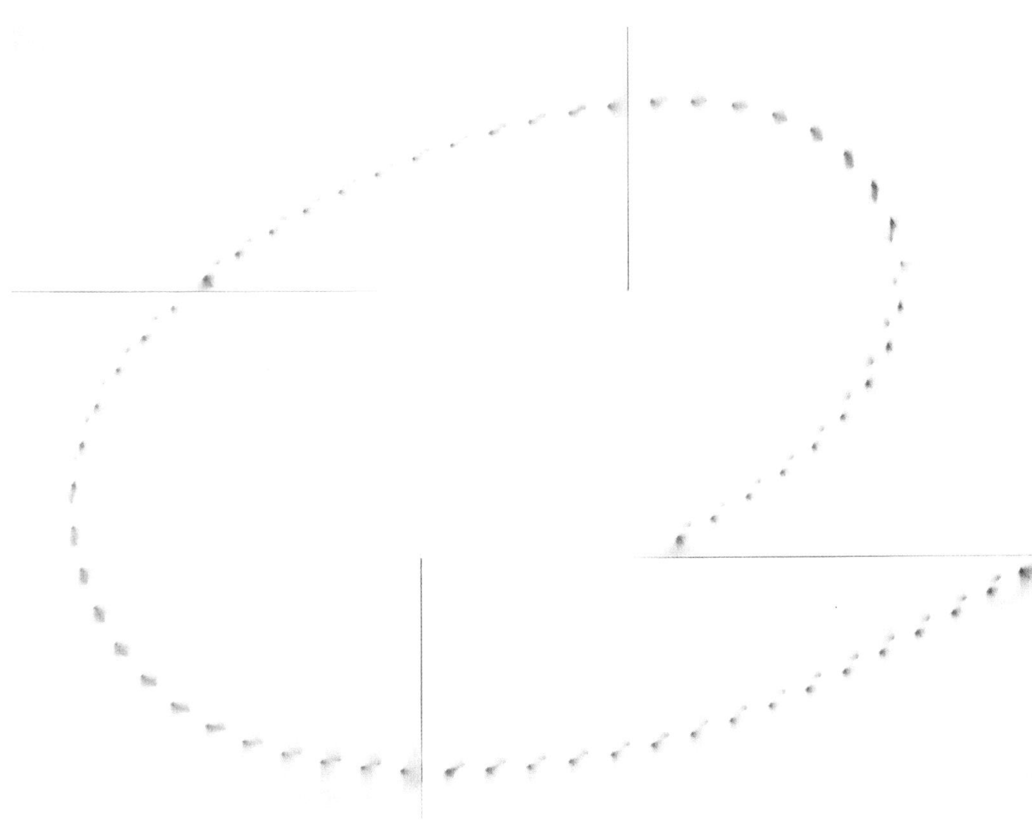

Agostino Bonalumi
Blu, 1972
vinyl-based tempera
on shaped canvas
180 × 160 cm / 70 ⅞ × 63 in

"The effect of tension [...] can always be felt in my works and [...], if there is opposition from the canvas-surface to the internal thrusting and pressure, it assumes the character of psychological tension to emerge in the abstraction of a morphism that is an intrusion of the natural. Tension that in abstraction is, once again, a symbolic impulse or drive, in other words, the natural that is the nature of the work beyond its mere objecthood."

– AGOSTINO BONALUMI

– "Scritto (1996)", in *Bonalumi*, exhibition catalogue, ed. by Alberto Fiz, Fabrizio Bonalumi, (Catanzaro, MARCA, 22 February - 31 May 2014), Silvana Editoriale, Milan, 2014, p. 200.

Paolo Scheggi
Intersuperficie curva bianca, 1967
acrylic on three superimposed canvases
140 × 140 × 7 cm / 55 ⅛ × 55 ⅛ × 2 ¾ in

"What you wrote is very intelligent in its logic. There may be differences between us, which I consider in your favor, you are a man of your time. I would only add that the arts are not 'only' one of the manifestations of intelligence, the reason for being 'human'. There can be no social evolution without a total evolution of mankind. I like your uneasiness, your quests, your paintings, so profoundly red, black, white, that indicate your thinking, your fear. I can only but wish you a 'happy' career and remind you to be humble, very humble. In time we are nothing."

– **LUCIO FONTANA**

– *Lucio Fontana's letter to Paolo Scheggi*, 1962. The letter refers to a self-introduction that Paolo Scheggi wrote for his second solo exhibition at the Galleria Il Cancello in Bologna.

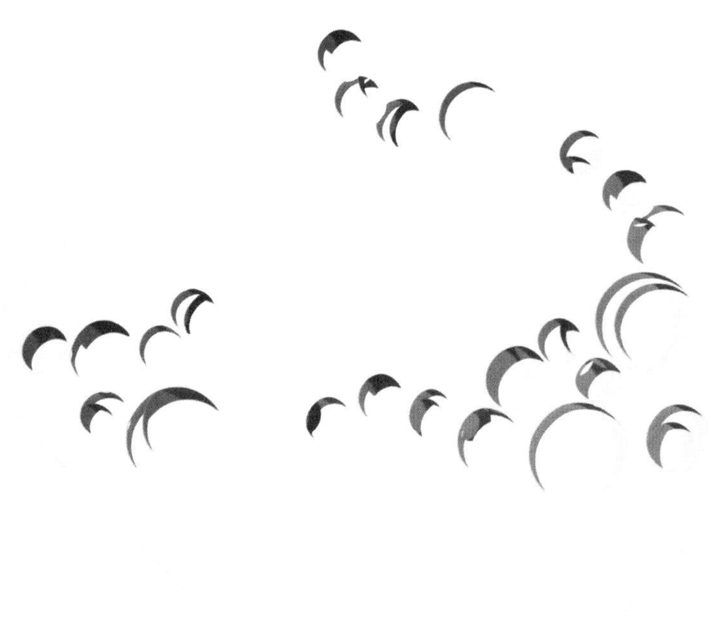

Dadamaino
Volume a moduli sfasati, 1960
perforated plastic on frame
100 × 70 cm / 39 ⅜ × 27 ½ in

"As simple, practical devices, subtly reminiscent of past creations, the *Volumi a moduli sfasati* had something of a 'do-it-yourself' quality to them, and they opened the artwork to unexplored dimensions. It was still 1960, plastic was not only used as a way to desacralize classic materials; it was also explored for its own potential and its intrinsic qualities. Working with plastic was Dadamaino's way of being 'absolutely modern' and of doing away with 'the ancient world' [...] the break was clear, and the year 1960, in that regard, marked a seminal moment. For Dadamaino, plastic is a material, which she uses rigorously, by following a method. Using tools that she borrowed from the industrial world, she continuously, regularly poked the canvas on all of its surface."

– BERNARD BLISTÈNE

– *Dadamaino*, exhibition catalogue, ed. by Bernard Blistène, (Paris, Tornabuoni Art, 11 October 2013 - 4 January 2014), Forma Edizioni, Florence, 2013, p. 21.

Dadamaino
Oggetto ottico-dinamico, 1962-71
milled aluminium plates on nylon threads on wood
106 × 106 cm / 41 ¾ × 41 ¾ in

"Space is a physical and mental *locus*, a condition of life. The work is something that passes through this locus and reworks it through a strongly sensitized perceptual maturity. The recurrent use of black and white replaces all the possibilities of color, almost as though the artist were concerned not to be distracted by the temptation to describe and narrate. Dadamaino's work remains an extreme gesture of total intensity and power. [...] The reiteration of action becomes almost obsessive, an obsession that paradoxically adds by subtracting, an insistence on serial form. This too is a form of linguistic cancellation."

– VITTORIA COEN

– *Minimalia. An Italian Vision in 20th-century Art*, exhibition catalogue, ed. by Achille Bonito Oliva, (New York, MoMA PS1 Contemporary Art Center, 10 October 1999 - 9 January 2000), Electa Edizioni, Milan, 1999, p. 71.

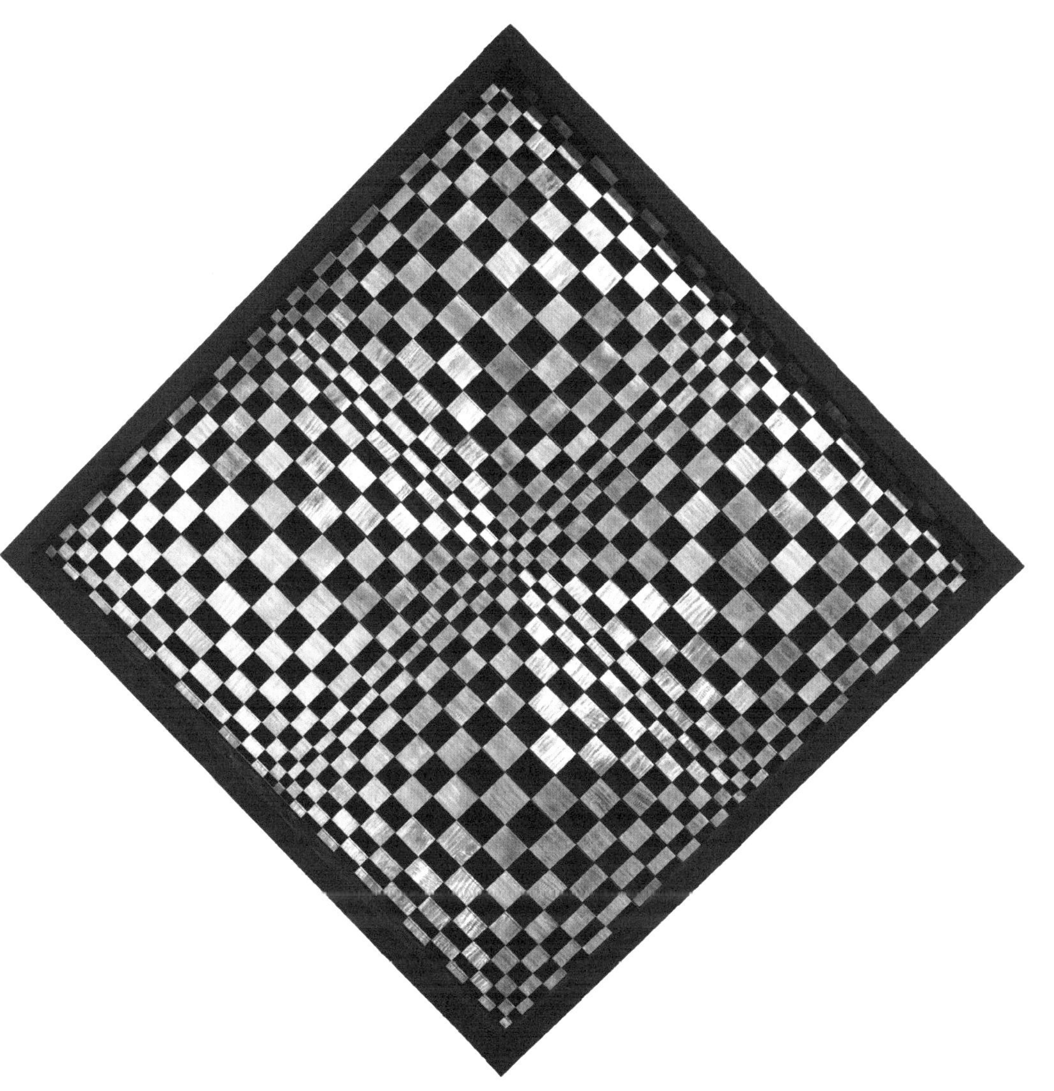

Gianni Colombo
Senza titolo, 1975
mixed media and collage on cardboard
67.5 × 51.6 cm / 26 ⅝ × 20 ¼ in

"I chose a practical cubic container as a field of representation: one of the habitable forms most usual for us, in which permutations of forms and dimensions unfold: a habitable condition most unusual for us."

– GIANNI COLOMBO

– Exhibition catalogue for the L'Attico gallery (Rome 1968). The text is dated Milan 1967.

Giuseppe Uncini
"Spazi di ferro" n°26 (rilievo), 1989
concrete and iron
150 × 194 × 30 cm / 59 × 76 ⅜ × 11 ¾ in

"As the artist himself declares, his work is composed of physical and non-physical materials, 'the body and logic of the idea'. Empty and occupied space, an essential master plan, light and shadow, and the colors of matter thus produce figures of a mainly two-dimensional nature, to be hung on the wall, endowed with their own static and hieratic physicality. In 1985, Uncini called them 'images' whose internal geometry serves as a vehicle of comprehension and not as a final objective.
From the late 1950s on, the artist's poetic course is one of personal investigation seeking to go beyond the Art-informel tradition towards a motivation more closely linked to ideas. The ideas in question took on social connotations in art, especially in the early sixties, in open dialogue with scientific research but in opposition to the sense of alienation of certain mechanistic attitudes tied up with a distorted idea of industrial progress."

– VITTORIA COEN

– *Minimalia. An Italian Vision in 20th-century Art*, exhibition catalogue, ed. by Achille Bonito Oliva, (New York, MoMA PS1 Contemporary Art Center, 10 October 1999 - 9 January 2000), Electa Edizioni, Milan, 1999.

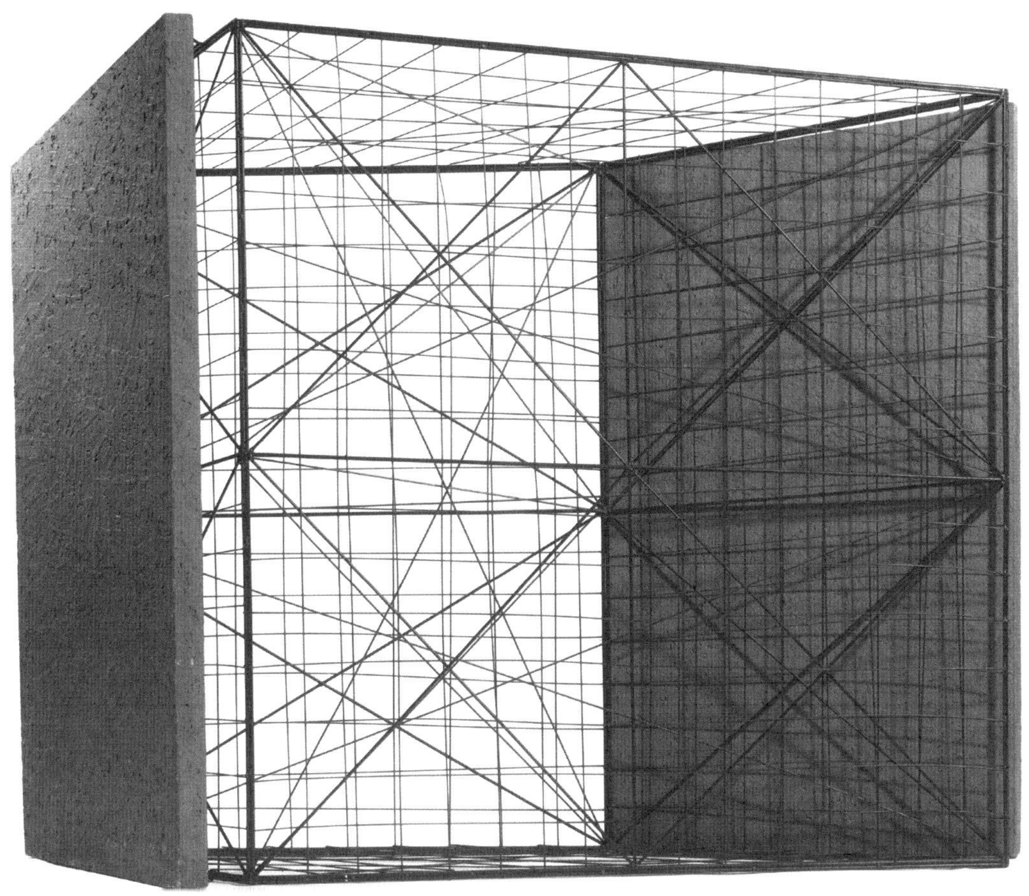

Sergio Lombardo
Bianco 77, 1961
enamel on wood
113 × 72 cm / 44 ½ × 28 ⅜ in

"In the *Monocromi* (Monochromes) of the early sixties the artist reduces composition to the bare minimum, and above all delegates it to a nearly automatic process. [...] An absolute dichromatic approach is sufficient to give us an immediate sense of absence, of a contrast that is between light and shadow even though its starting point is of a 'political' nature."

– VITTORIA COEN

– *Minimalia. An Italian Vision in 20th-century Art*, exhibition catalogue, ed. by Achille Bonito Oliva, (New York, MoMA PS1 Contemporary Art Center, 10 October 1999 - 9 January 2000), Electa Edizioni, Milan, 1999, p. 80.

Alighiero Boetti
Titoli, 1978
embroidery on cloth
172 × 178 cm / 67 ¾ × 70 ⅛ in

"His work was always linked to an object, to an idea, to a concept that exhausted its formal justification while engendering a play of intellectual reflections that were specific to the idea. I've always appreciated the lively intelligence behind his inventions. His works often give the idea that they'll be exhausted by the logic of their presence but their continuity and, when combined together, their obsession reveal his need to rationalise existence."

– GIUSEPPE PENONE

– Andrea Bellini, Giuseppe Penone, "Conversation avec Giuseppe Penone", in *Alighiero Boetti,* ed. by Laura Cherubini, Forma Edizioni, Florence, 2016, p. 186.

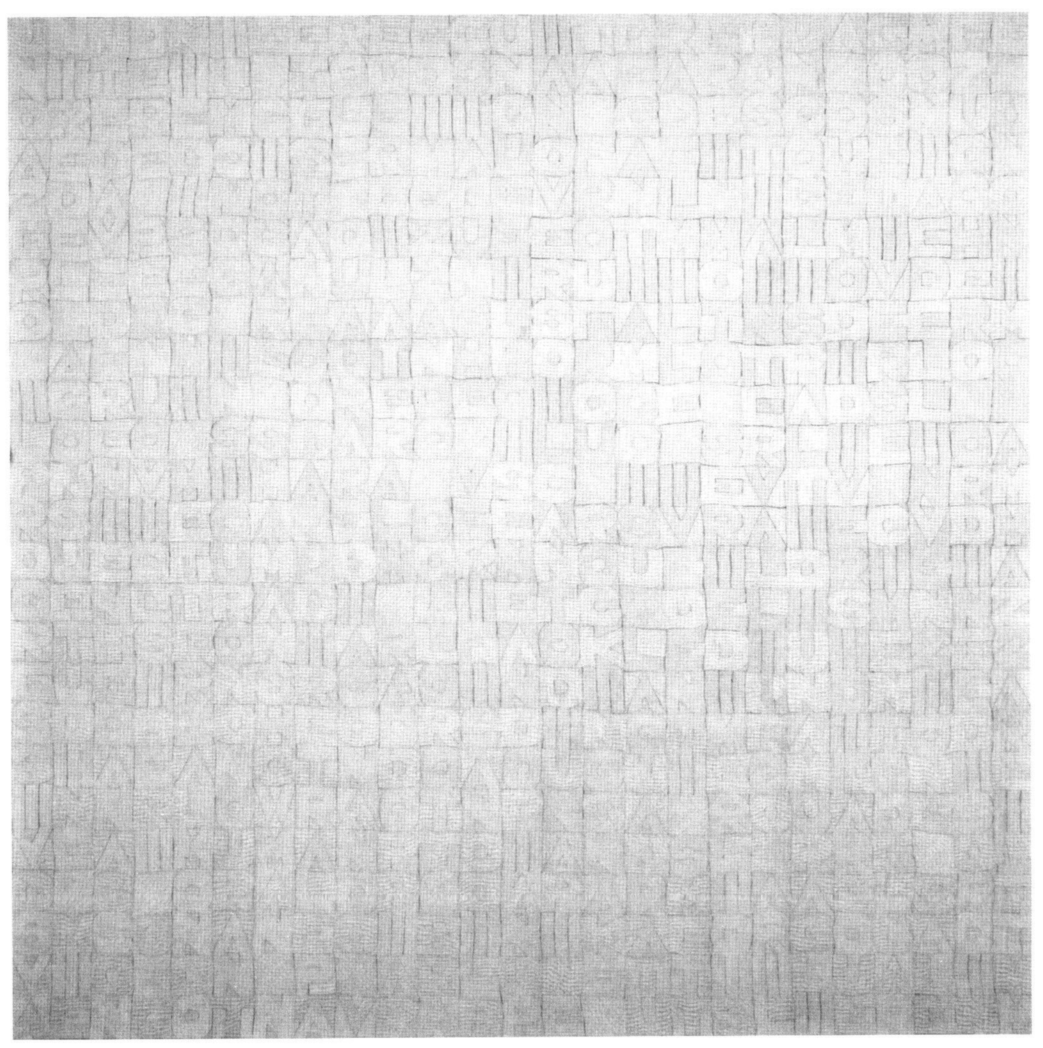

Alighiero Boetti
Catasta, 1967-92
12 elements in Eternit
187 × 150 × 150 cm / 73 ⅝ × 59 × 59 in

"Closer in spirit to Carl Andre's notion that 'A man climbs a mountain because it's there. A man makes a work of art because it isn't there', Boetti in fact made objects precisely because their elements were already there, and their choice and assembly constituted only the smallest act of creation."

– CHRISTIAN RATTEMEYER

– *Alighiero Boetti: Game Plan*, exhibition catalogue, (Madrid, Museo Nacional de Arte Reina Sofia; London, Tate Modern; New York, The Museum of Modern Art), Tate Publishing, London, 2012, p. 30.

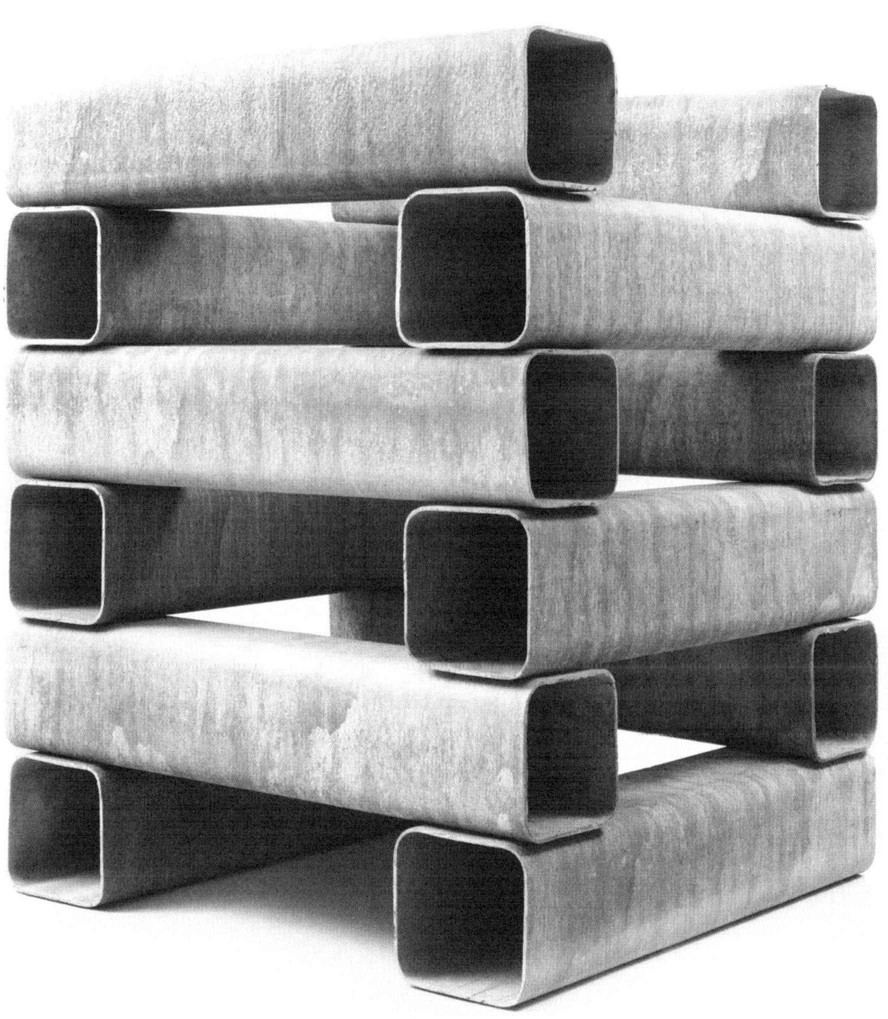

Mario Ceroli
Senza titolo, 1971
Russian pine wood
145 × 105 × 21 cm /
57 ⅛ × 41 ⅜ × 8 ¼ in

"During the sixties Ceroli was one of the first artists in Italy to address the problem of the work of art and its relation to its environment, both internal and external, which acts as an enormous stage enabling human figures and things to take shape gradually, to come to life through fluid forms that become the shadows and projections of our thoughts. [...] Spatial aspiration appears to be a primary need of these works. Each of them acquires greater meaning through the location and emphasis derived by the structures from depth and the play of shadows arising from it."

– VITTORIA COEN

– *Minimalia. An Italian Vision in 20th-century Art*, exhibition catalogue, ed. by Achille Bonito Oliva, (New York, MoMA PS1 Contemporary Art Center, 10 October 1999 - 9 January 2000), Electa Edizioni, Milan, 1999, p. 68.

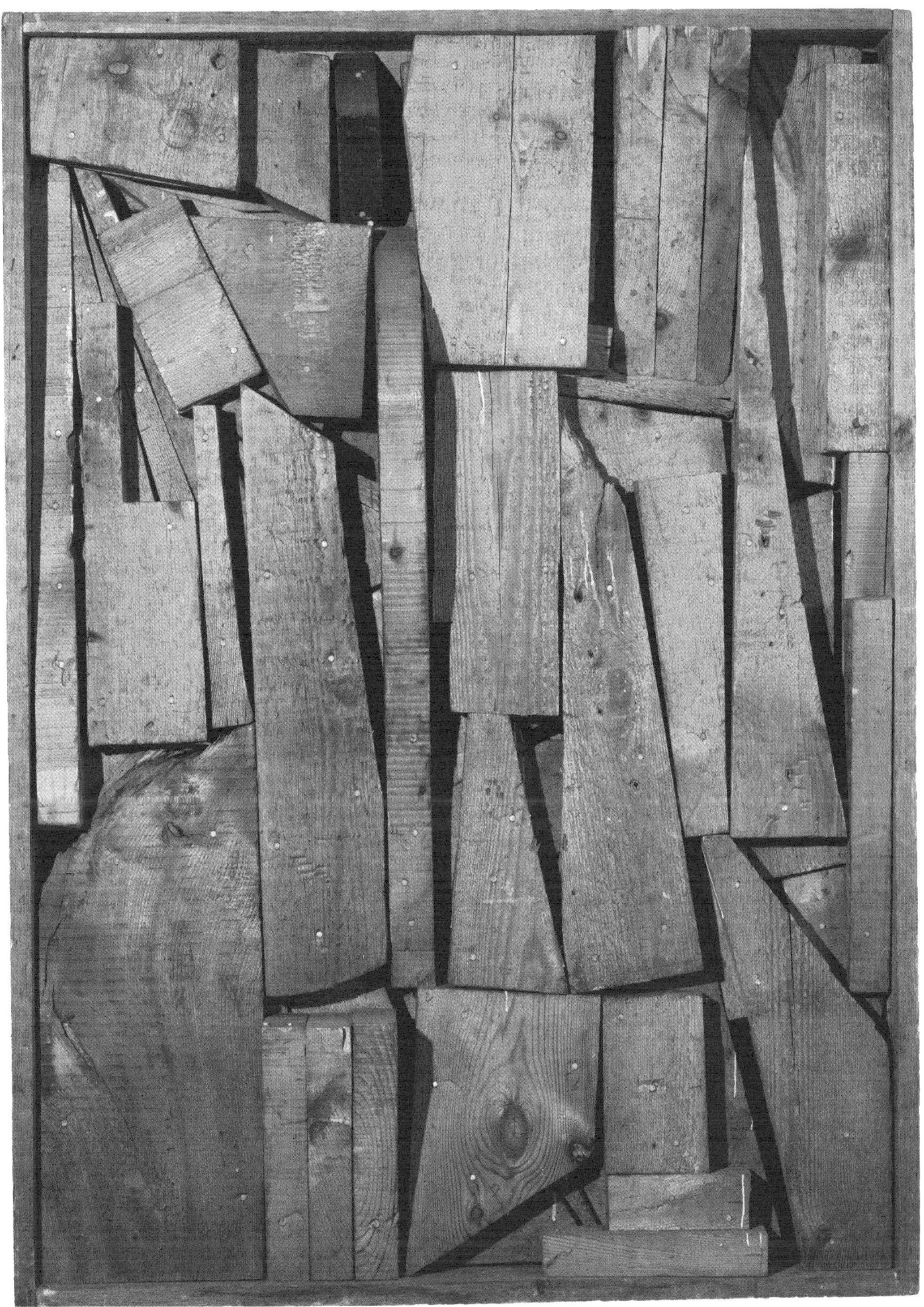

Jannis Kounellis
Senza titolo, 1989
iron and lead
183 × 206 × 12 cm /
72 × 81 ⅛ × 4 ¾ in

"The industrial materials [which Kounellis] uses are a transcription of an old story; he puts an *Ur-Sprache* (Original language) to a contemporary use, something one has not failed to relate to his Greek origins. The proportions of the steel plates he uses in his works only become clear when one realizes that they actually correspond to those of a double bed. As Kounellis himself writes, 'I have not wanted anything but very beautiful things. I have seen the sacred in objects of everyday use. I have believed in weight as only a measure. I want to bring about a return of poetry, with every means: with exercise, observation, solitude, the word, the image'."

– DANIEL ABADIE

– *Tout Feu tout Flamme*, ed. by Daniel Abadie, (Paris, Tornabuoni Art, 5 October - 22 December 2012), Forma Edizioni, Florence, 2012.

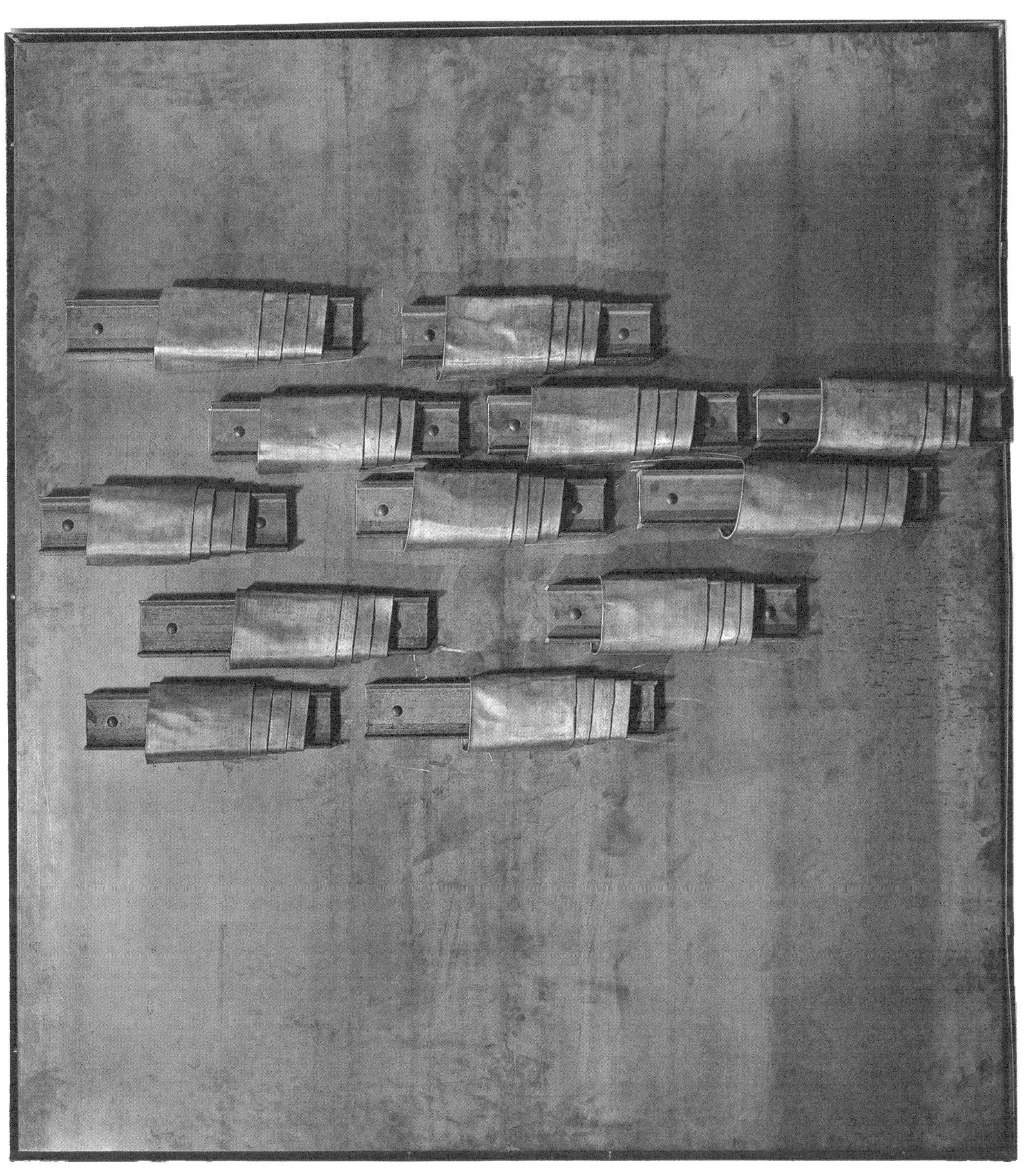

Vincenzo Agnetti
Assioma: l'opposizione è un riflesso gli opposti si equivalgono, 1970
black bakelite, white nitro paint
70 × 70 cm / 27 ½ × 27 ½ in

"If one uses whichever language or discipline to make art, they will soon find themselves forced to reset the discipline itself, to take it back to the starting point. That will be the moment to exploit the chosen discipline until its structure is eradicated. The concepts will then be reduced to pure and simple signals: when looked at all together, these signals will create a composition, in a way an equivalent of signs and colors in oil paintings."

– VINCENZO AGNETTI

– *Letter to Françoise Lambert*, December 1971, in occasion of the exhibition *Spazio perduto spazio costruito 8 proposizioni* then published in *Domus* at the beginning of 1972.

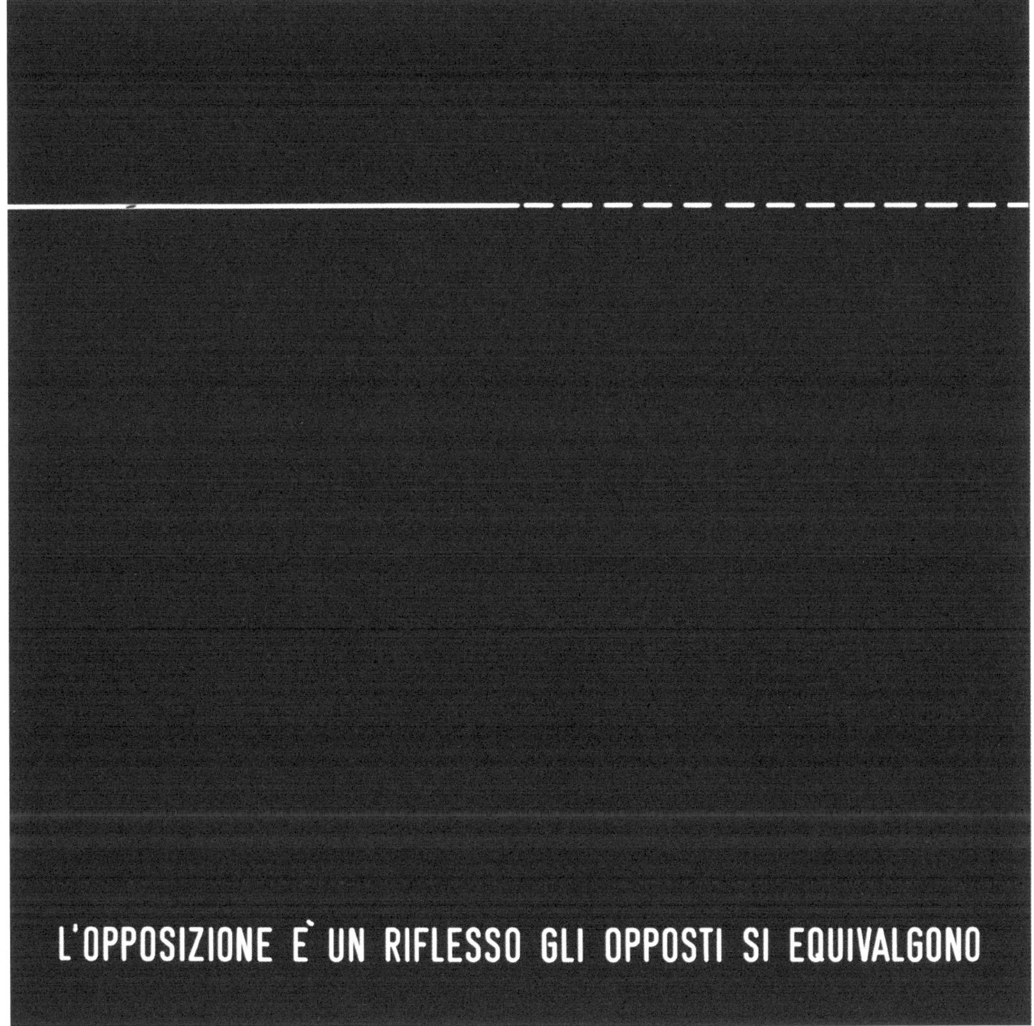
L'OPPOSIZIONE È UN RIFLESSO GLI OPPOSTI SI EQUIVALGONO

Emilio Isgrò
Il braccio, 1985
mixed media on canvas on wood
118 × 200 cm / 46 ½ × 78 ¾ in

"The exact opposite of the Baroque *horror vacui* (fear of emptiness) is Isgrò's declared detachment from the traditional preoccupation of occupying and dominating the natural body of things. He initially used scraps of phrases in jumbled sequences that did not strip them of meaning but went beyond their typographical structure to marshal them as the minimal component of a literal sign. He then went on to produce panels made illegible by repeated cancellation. Eliminating any illusion of the possibility of conveying a message through words, conceptualizing an approach glimpsed in the realm of the concrete, and extricating himself from the impasse of prioritizing the elements to be used, he freely manipulated the codes of transmission."

– VITTORIA COEN

– *Minimalia. An Italian Vision in 20th-century Art*, exhibition catalogue, ed. by Achille Bonito Oliva, (New York, MoMA PS1 Contemporary Art Center, 10 October 1999 - 9 January 2000), Electa Edizioni, Milan, 1999, p. 79.

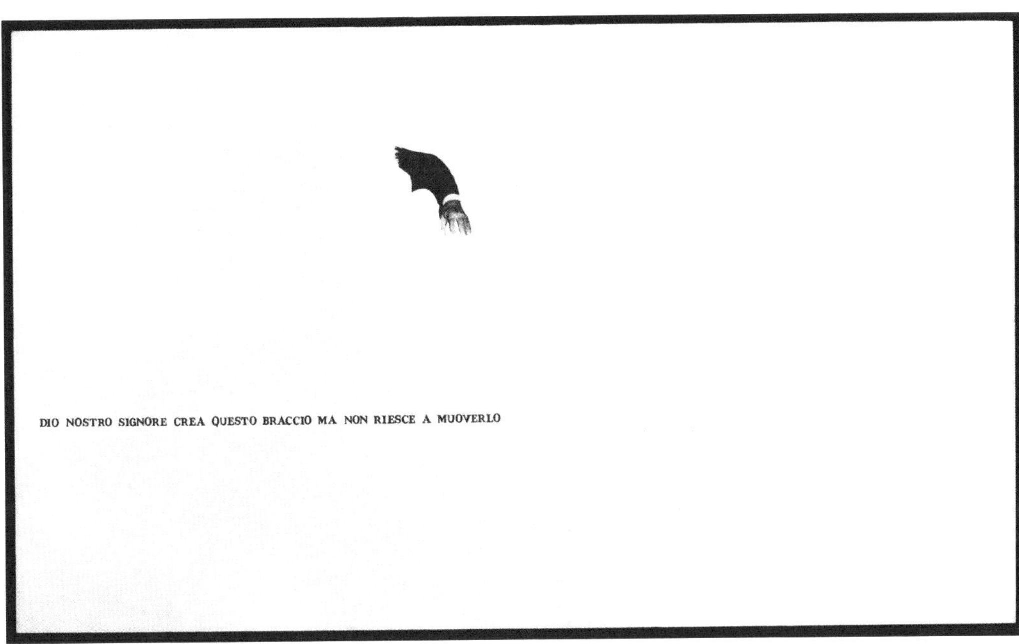
DIO NOSTRO SIGNORE CREA QUESTO BRACCIO MA NON RIESCE A MUOVERLO

BIOGRAPHIES

Vincenzo Agnetti
[Milan, 1926 - 1981]

After graduating from the Accademia delle Belle Arti di Brera, Agnetti studied dramaturgy at the school of the Piccolo Teatro in Milan. His first paintings date from the late 1940's and over the following decade they were mostly influenced by the Informal movement. Although the expressive impact characteristic of that movement corresponded to his own quest for immediacy, he soon realized how challenging it would be to achieve plenitude through painting. From then on he focused on language and became closer to Enrico Castellani and Piero Manzoni, with whom he founded the journal *Azimuth*. In 1962, Agnetti decided to take some distance, intellectually as well as geographically, and he voluntarily decided to lose himself and to disappear from the world for a while: he left for South America, the Arctic and Arabia, a phase that he himself defined as "arte-no". Upon his return, in 1967, he got in touch with the Milanese artistic scene again and quickly published *Obsoleto*, an "anti-novel" that he had written between 1963 and 1965, in which he deconstructed the logical structures of narration, syntax and grammar. His first solo exhibition was held the same year at the Palazzo dei Diamanti in Ferrara, where he showed *Principia*, one of his "permutable logic" work. In 1970 he created the NEG, in collaboration with Brionvega. That work was emblematic of Agnetti's work; it used the musical pauses and micro-intervals that separated sounds coming from a record-player – in other words the perception of silence, which he called *suono bianco* (white sound). Vincenzo Agnetti died in Milan in 1981.

Alighiero Boetti
[Turin, 1940 - Rome, 1994]

Self-taught, he is quickly linked to the Arte Povera and presents his first solo exhibitions in 1967 (Galleria Christian Stein, Turin, Galleria La Bertesca, Genoa). In 1972, he played with the symmetry of the double, under the names of Alighiero and Boetti. From 1971 to 1979, he made many trips to Afghanistan and began a cycle of colorful embroideries realised by Afghan women. A frequent traveller, Boetti lived in many countries and his travels were the inspiration for many of his works, including *Lavori Postali*, a series created with postage stamps. Using letters, maps, and numbers, he designed new mechanisms based on mathematical rules and infinite combinations. Starting in 1972, he exhibited often at the Venice Biennale and the Kassel Documenta. He presented major solo exhibitions around the world and is now considered a leading source of inspiration for successive generations of artists.

Agostino Bonalumi
[Vimercate, 1936 - Desio, 2013]

At a very young age he started frequenting artistic circles in Milan and he became a regular at Enrico Baj's studio, where he met Piero Manzoni and Enrico Castellani, who became his close friends. Bonalumi also contributed to the *Azimuth* journal and gallery (Azimut), both founded in 1959 by Castellani and Manzoni. In 1961, he was among the founders of Nouvelle Ecole Européenne, and he later joined the Zero group with whom he exhibited in 1965. In the early 1960's he created his monochromatic and *estroflesse* (extroflexed) canvases, which, according to various techniques, tended to create light and shadow effects; they were often coined "object-paintings" and came to define his style. Towards the end of that decade he created the first works that combined space and painting, called *Ambienti* (Spaces), which became his signature pieces. In 1965, Arturo Schwarz organized a solo exhibition for the artist in his gallery in Milan, with a foreword by Gillo Dorfles, an internationally renowned Milanese critic, who later followed Bonalumi's work consistently throughout the painter's career. In 1966 he was invited to show his works for the first time at the Venice Biennial, where an entire room was dedicated to his work in 1970. In 1980, an important retrospective, organized at the Palazzo Te in Mantua, proposed an analytical journey throughout the main periods of his career. In 2001 the Accademia Nazionale di San Luca awarded him the Premio Presidente della Repubblica for sculpture, and the following year he created *Ambiente Bianco – Spazio trattenuto e spazio invaso* for the Peggy Guggenheim Foundation in Venice.

Alberto Burri
[Città di Castello, 1915 - Nice, 1995]

He trained as a doctor, before being called up for duty in the Italian army. Captured in Tunisia in 1943, he was sent to a prisoner-of-war camp in Texas, where he rediscovered his passion for art. His work is quickly defined by the use of unorthodox materials and techniques: he worked with tar, Vinavil or sand, followed by

jute in 1949. In 1952, he created his first *Sacchi*. The Solomon R. Guggenheim Museum in New York presented it to the American public during a collective exhibition in 1953, thus consecrating it as a major artist of the avant-garde scene. The exhibition was quickly followed by his first monograph (1955). The same year, the discovery of fire as a means of creation had important consequences for his production, and therefore defines almost all his main series.
Burri participated in the Venice Biennale in 1952, and three major exhibitions were dedicated to his art at the National Museum of Modern Art in Paris (1972), the Tate Gallery in London (1974) and the Museo Nazionale d'Arte Moderna in Rome (1976). More recently, important retrospectives were organised by the Solomon R. Guggenheim Museum in New York (2016) and by the Fondazione Cini in Venice (2019), in collaboration with Tornabuoni Art.

Enrico Castellani
[Castelmassa, 1930 - Viterbo, 2017]

He moved to Brussels in 1952, attended the Royal Academy of Fine Arts and the Ecole Nationale Supérieure where he graduated as an architect in 1956. He returned to live in Milan where he founded the magazine *Azimuth* (1959) and the gallery of the same name with Piero Manzoni. The group fought against Informal Art and for the creation of a new pictorial language. Castellani rejected mimetic art, claiming that light, shadow or space must be contained in the work itself without being represented using descriptive means. In this context, he realized his *Superficie*, which consists of monochrome canvases, sunken or raised with nails placed behind the frame. These works of a radical novelty are considered fundamental for the artistic history of the twentieth century: Castellani has notably influenced the artist Donald Judd, who saw him as the father of Minimalism. In 1960, he participated in the *Monochrome Malerei* exhibition at the Kunstmuseum in Leverkusen, Germany. Other important exhibitions follow in the world, including the Venice Biennale (1964, 1968) and the Kassel Documenta (1968).

Mario Ceroli
[Castel Frentano, 1938]

Self-taught, the artist quickly gained international recognition: he won the Youth Prize for Sculpture at the National Gallery of Modern and Contemporary Art in Rome (1958) and the Venice Biennale Prize for Sculpture (1966) for his work *Cassa Sistina*, nowadays in the collection of the Centre Pompidou in Paris. Ceroli advocates a return to the origins of manual creation, the rediscovery of the *homo faber*, able to give shape to an idea through the craft industry. During a trip to Assisi in 1957, he discovered the art of Giotto, an experience that inspired him his first wooden silhouette. His art is not limited to sculpture and his interest in various disciplines pushes him to experiment with performing arts, including theatre and opera, for which he designed several sets (Scala Milan, Fenice Venice, Bolshoi Moscow). In the 1970s and 80s, he also experimented with marble, glass and bronze, revisiting canonical works of painting and sculpture from the Renaissance to the present day. He lives and works in Rome.

Gianni Colombo
[Milan, 1937 - Melzo, 1993]

He founded the Gruppo T (with Anceschi, Boriani and De Vecchi) in 1959 and he joined the international movement New Tendencies. As a leading representative of the kinetic and programmed art experiments, he presented his first solo exhibition at Galleria Pater (Milan, 1960). In the 1960s, he made art and experimental films, kinetic objects and interior designs. From the 1980s, he created avant-garde scenographies (Open theater, Frankfurt, 1986) and designed virtual architectures. He exhibited his work on numerous occasions in Italy and abroad (First Prize for Painting, Venice Biennale, 1968). He taught at the Brera Academy, where he became director in 1985.

Dadamaino
[Milan, 1930 - 2004]

Born Eduarda Emilia Maino, Dadamaino became acquainted with the art world when she met the post-war Milanese avant-garde, at the end of the 1950s. She immediately joined the Azimuth group and the Zero group and developed her own personal vision inspired by Lucio Fontana's Spatialism. Her work was soon exposed throughout Europe. With Getulio Alviani, Bruno Munari and Enzo Mari, she was one of the founders of the movement New Tendencies, and participated in numerous exhibitions around the world as part of that group. She gradually organised her work around a visual alphabet of sixteen signs, which she called "mental alphabet". She was invited to exhibit her work at the Venice Biennale (1980, 1990) and her works are nowadays housed in many collections such as the Tate Modern in London, the Solomon R. Guggenheim Foundation in Venice, the Foundation of Concrete Art in Reutlingen in Germany and the Centre Pompidou in Paris.

Lucio Fontana
[Rosario Santa Fe, 1899 - Comabbio, 1968]

Born in Argentina, Fontana was the founder of Spatialism, an aesthetic movement that he pioneered in his *Manifiesto Blanco* (1946). His "spatial" research focused on imparting a third dimension to his paintings by treating them as sculptures. Characterised by holes or slashes, his series of monochrome paintings entitled *Concetto Spaziale* epitomises this radical work for which he has gained international recognition.
He often collaborated with architects (with Baldessari: staircase of honor, Triennale di Milano, 1951, Breda Pavilion, Fair of Milan, 1952). In his lifetime, his work was exhibited at the Venice Biennale (1966), where he won the first prize for painting, and at the MoMA in New York (1966). He has been the subject of many exhibitions since then, notably a retrospective at the Musée d'Art Moderne de la Ville de Paris in 2014 and at the Met Breuer, New York, in 2019.

Jannis Kounellis
[Piraeus, 1936 - Rome, 2017]

At the age of 19 Jannis Kounellis moved to Italy and settled in Rome, where he attended the Fine Arts Academy. Through his artistic training, Kounellis considered himself a champion of Italian culture, that of Titian's *Madonna*, which he perceived as a revolutionary symbol. At the end of the 1950s, he created a poetic language based on a combination of elementary language units such as letters and symbols, painted on white canvas with black tempera, which became the subject of his first exhibition at Galleria della Tartaruga in Rome. In 1967 he exhibited with artists of the Arte Povera movement at the L'Attico gallery in Rome, where he showed one of his most famous pieces: an installation featuring 12 living horses. Over the next ten years, he introduced humble materials in his work, such as burlap, coal, wax, iron, lead and wool, combining them with live natural elements such as animals or plants. Kounellis wanted to invent a new form of language in which nature, culture and life could communicate. In 1972, he exhibited at Documenta 5 in Kassel and at the Venice Biennale. Kounellis' work became gradually more performative, taking on a more theatrical and musical dimension – he also designed several opera sets. During the last years of his career the artist explored his original themes, moving towards a monumentality that echoes his early large-scale urban projects. Jannis Kounellis died in 2017 in Rome at the age of 80.

Emilio Isgrò
[Barcellona di Sicilia, 1937]

An artist but also a poet and a writer, Isgrò is one of the pioneers of the "*cancellatura*" (deletion) which he experimented since the sixties and which still holds today its power and creative audacity. He moved to Milan in 1956, where he made his literary debut with a collection of poems entitled *Fiere del Sud*. In 1964, the artist produced his first *Cancellature*, erasing the words Encyclopedia letting show only fragments of the text, therefore contributing to the rise of visual poetry and conceptual art. Subsequently the artist will apply this deletion to geographical maps, images and music score, while creating conceptual installations. Isgrò's art is at the intersection of presence and absence, deconstruction and reconstruction, offering a new meaning to the media on which he intervenes. During the 1960s Isgrò exhibited in Milan, Genova, Bologna and Naples, he also participated in several editions of the Venice Biennale: 1972, 1978, 1986 and 1993. In 1977 he was awarded with the prize of the XIV Biennale d'Arte de São Paulo in Brazil. In 1989 he created a new *Teoria della cancellatura* and took part in the exhibition The Artist and the Book in Twentieth-Century Italy, presented in 1992-1993 at the MoMA in New York and in 1994 at the Peggy Guggenheim Collection in Venice.

Sergio Lombardo
[Rome, 1939]

After classical and law studies, he dedicated himself to artistic research and experimental psychology of aesthetics. He made his debut as an artist in the early sixties together with the protagonists of the New Roman School supported by the Galleria della Tartaruga exhibiting with Rotella, Kounellis, Schifano, Festa, Angeli, Mambor, Tacchi, Ceroli and Pascali. He later joined the group of the La Salita gallery exhibiting with Burri, Fontana, Lo Savio, Manzoni, Paolini and Mochetti. In 1970 he exhibited at the Italian pavilion of the Venice Biennale and in the early seventies, he devoted himself to postmodernism and the global entertainment society. He founded the self-managed Jartrakor gallery and the Art Psychology Magazine, giving life to the eventualist movement. Since the 1980s, he has developed *Stocastica* painting, automatic artistic creation procedures. He exhibits in numerous exhibitions including a personal exhibition in 2004 at the Mudima Foundation of Milan and in 2011 at the collective Italian Masterpieces a look at the twentieth century at the Museum of modern and contemporary art of Trento and Rovereto. His works have been exhibited at the National Museum of Modern Art in Tokyo (1967), at the Jewish Museum of New York (1968), at the Center Georges Pompidou in Paris (1969, 1995), and many others. He currently works on Toroidal Minimal Maps and Heawood Maps.

Piero Manzoni
[Soncino, 1933 - Milan, 1963]

He attended the Brera Academy for a short period of time. In 1957, he adheres to Nuclear Movement for which he signs the programmatic documents and makes his first *Achromes*. Critic and engaged theorist in contact with the Zero group, he founded the magazine *Azimuth* (1959) and the eponymous gallery with Enrico Castellani. In 1960, he signed the manifesto *Du rien contre le rien*, he participated at the exhibition *Monochrome Malerei* (Kunstmuseum, Leverkusen, near Cologne) and he organised the event *Consumazione dell'arte dinamica del pubblico divorare arte* (Azimut gallery). From 1957 he presents his series *Linee, Corpi d'aria, Fiato d'artista, Uova scultura, Basi magiche, Achromes, Sculture viventi, Merda d'artista* in numerous solo and collective exhibitions around the world, ahead of the trends of Arte Povera and Conceptual Art.

Paolo Scheggi
[Florence, 1940 - Rome, 1971]

Scheggi was a multidisciplinary artist who worked in visual arts, architecture, fashion, poetry and performance, revealing an approach that was both conceptual and metaphysical. His artistic attitude brought him closer to Bonalumi, Manzoni and Castellani, and led him to build on this principle of "object-painting" by questioning visual perceptions, and reinterpreting both Spatialism and monochrome painting. In 1965, he joined the New Tendencies movement and was in contact with the Zero group and Nul. In 1966 he was the youngest Italian artist at the Venice Biennale and in the same year he was invited to *Weiss auf Weiss* at the Kunsthalle in Bern, and at the XXI Salon des Réalités Nouvelles at the Musée d'Art Moderne in Paris. Fundamental is the architectural and environmental direction that his research has taken since 1964, working with Nizzoli Associati and Bruno Munari, and resulting in the *Intercamera plastica* conceived in the summer of 1966 and presented in Milan at the Galleria del Naviglio in January 1967. Since 1968 his investigation has been developing in a theatrical and performative direction, facing the overcoming of the traditional space of the scene and the gallery and extending into the city. The last two years have seen him engaged in conceptual and metaphysical research, aimed at investigating mythical-political language. Despite his very short life, he exhibited in the main artistic events of the time, from Paris to Buenos Aires, from New York to Hamburg, from Düsseldorf to Zagreb. In 2019, two major exhibitions are dedicated to him: at the Estorick Collection of Modern Italian Art, London, and the Museum of Contemporary Art in Zagreb, Croatia.

Giuseppe Uncini
[Fabriano, 1929 - Trevi, 2008]

A sculptor and painter, Giuseppe Uncini was trained at the Art Institute of Urbino and moved to Rome in 1953 where he took part of the artistic panorama of the city, knowing among others Capogrossi, Afro, Cagli. In 1955 he was invited to participate in the Rome Quadrennial. The following year he began the cycle of works called *Terre* using materials such as tuff, sand and ash. In 1957, his research shifted to materials such as iron and concrete, with which he realized the first Cementarmati which will become the stylistic code of his production. In 1961 he obtained his first solo exhibition at the L'Attico gallery in Rome. In 1962, together with Biggi, Carrino, Frascà, Pace and Santoro, he set up Group Uno for a valorization of the social role in art. The 1960s are characterized by his series *Ferrocementi*, where cement is smoothed to the point of losing its material quality and iron becomes the real protagonist of the work, determining the thickness of the cement layer. In 1966 he was invited to the Venice Biennale, where he exhibited the *Strutturespazio*. Uncini, thinking about the relationship between objects and shadows, developed a new series of works that reach architectural dimensions and that have their best example in Porta aperta con ombra, commissioned by Palma Bucarelli for the National Gallery of Modern Art in Rome. The last work created by Giuseppe Uncini is Epistylium, a sculpture in reinforced concrete over six meters high, and made for the Mart of Rovereto.

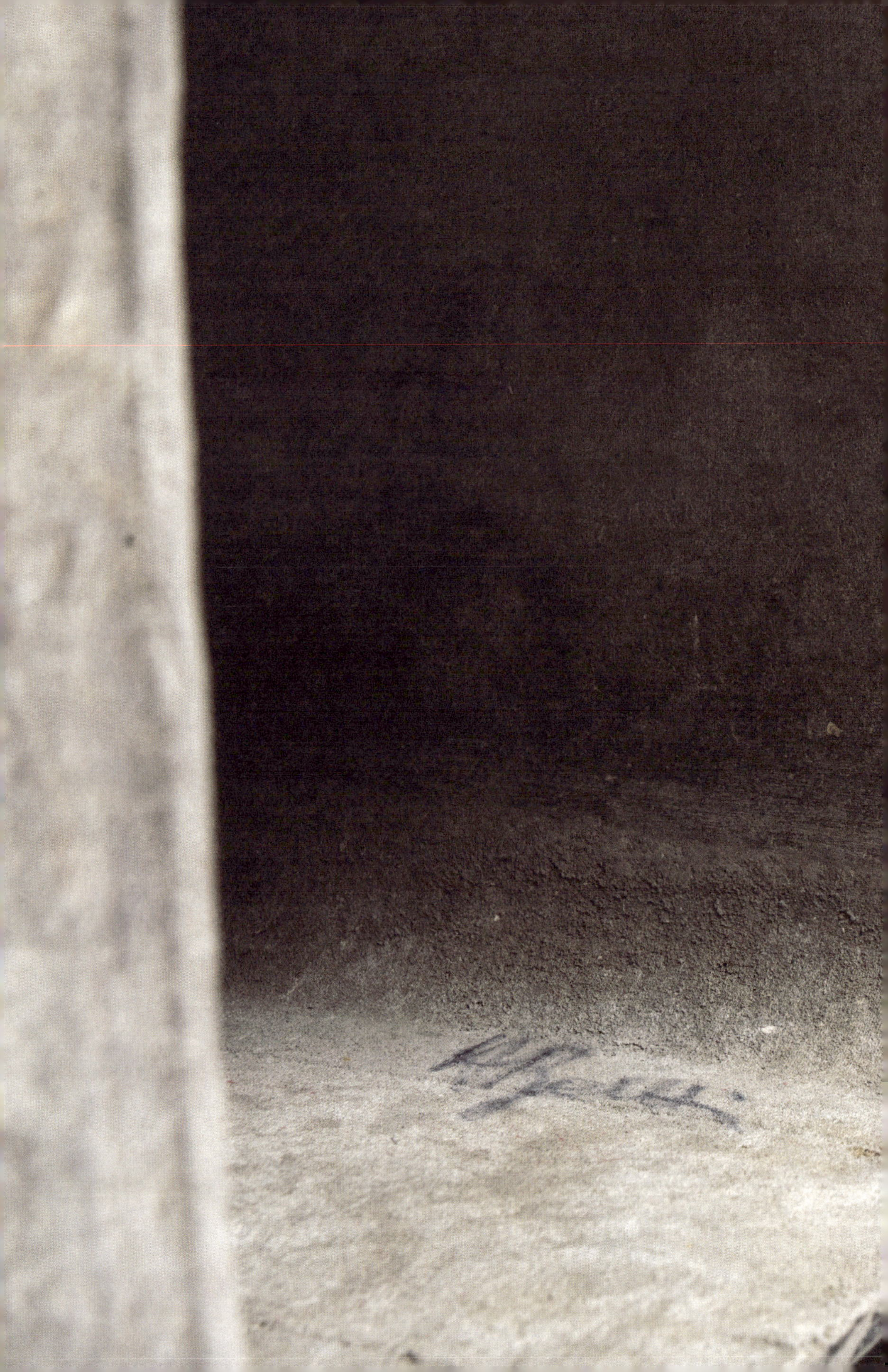

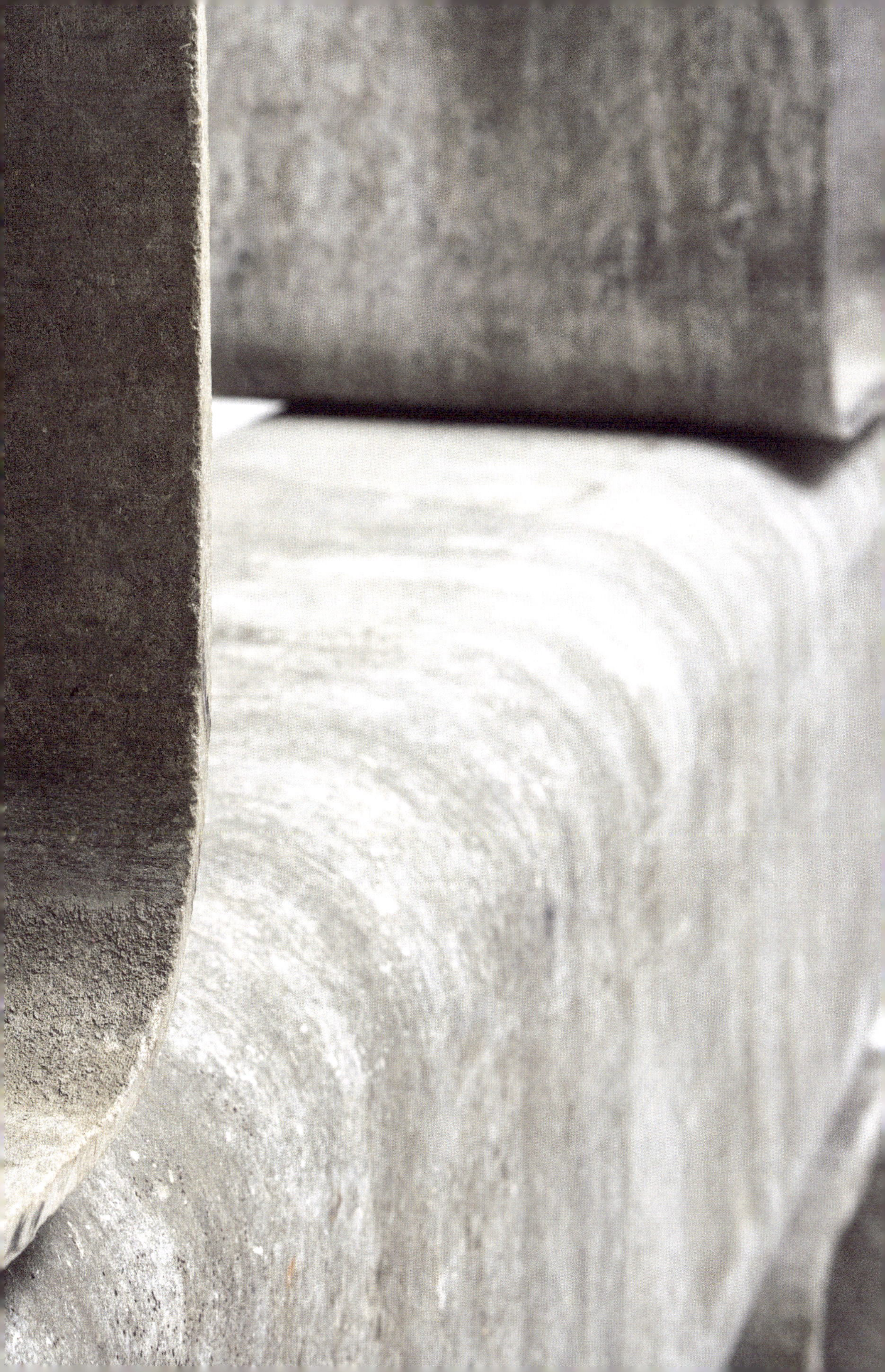

This volume was printed
in October 2020 by
Lito Terrazzi, Florence, Italy